Accidental Genius

Science Puzzles for Clever Kids

PENGUINS, POLAR BEARS, WALRUSES, and YAKS

The Arctic and Antarctic Biomes

Alix Wood

WINDMILL BOOKS

Published in 2024 by Windmill Books,
an Imprint of Rosen Publishing
2544 Clinton Street
Buffalo, NY 14224

Written, designed and illustrated by Alix Wood
All other images © AdobeStock Images

Cataloging-in-Publication Data

Names: Wood, Alix.
Title: Penguins, polar bears, walruses, and yaks: the arctic and antarctic biomes / Alix Wood.
Description: Buffalo, New York : Windmill Books, 2024. | Series: Accidental genius | Includes glossary and index.
Identifiers: ISBN 9781538394847 (pbk.) | ISBN 9781538394854 (library bound) | ISBN 9781538394861 (ebook)
Subjects: LCSH: Arctic regions--Juvenile literature. | Antarctica--Juvenile literature. | Games--Juvenile literature. | Picture puzzles--Juvenile literature.
Classification: LCC G614.W66 2024 | DDC 909'.0913--dc23

Printed in the United States of America

CPSIA Compliance Information: Batch CSWM24
For Further Information contact Rosen Publishing at 1-800-237-9932

Find us on

Contents

The Cold Poles....................................4
The Arctic 6
What Animals Live in the Arctic?.....8
Adaptable Animals..............................10
The Arctic Ocean 12
Big, Blubbery Walruses 14
Summer and Winter..............................16
Arctic Whales.................................... 18
Hunting Skills 20
Summer Tundra 22
Big, Hairy Cattle 24
The Antarctic 26
An Icy Desert 28
The Southern Ocean 30
Polar Science Stations 32
Great Penguin Dads............................34
Blue Whales 36
Humpback Whales 38
Glaciers and Icebergs 40
Protect the Poles!..............................42
Polar Biome Genius Test 44
Answers 46

The Cold Poles

The Arctic and Antarctic biomes are at the top and bottom of our planet. These areas are the coldest places on Earth because they are farthest from the sun.

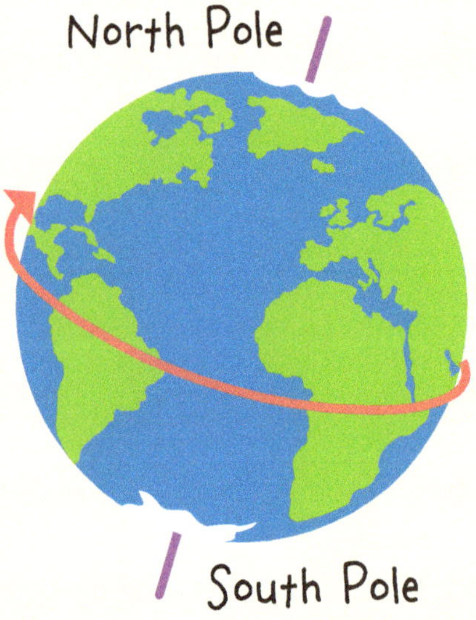

North Pole, South Pole

Imagine a stick stuck through Earth. Earth spins around the stick as it travels around the sun. Where the stick would poke out of the top is the North Pole. Where it would stick out of the bottom is the South Pole.

What are biomes? Biomes are areas with similar weather and temperature. Each type of biome is home to the plants and animals that can survive in those conditions.

Connect the Dots

Using tracing paper, connect the dots to find the animal the Arctic is named after.

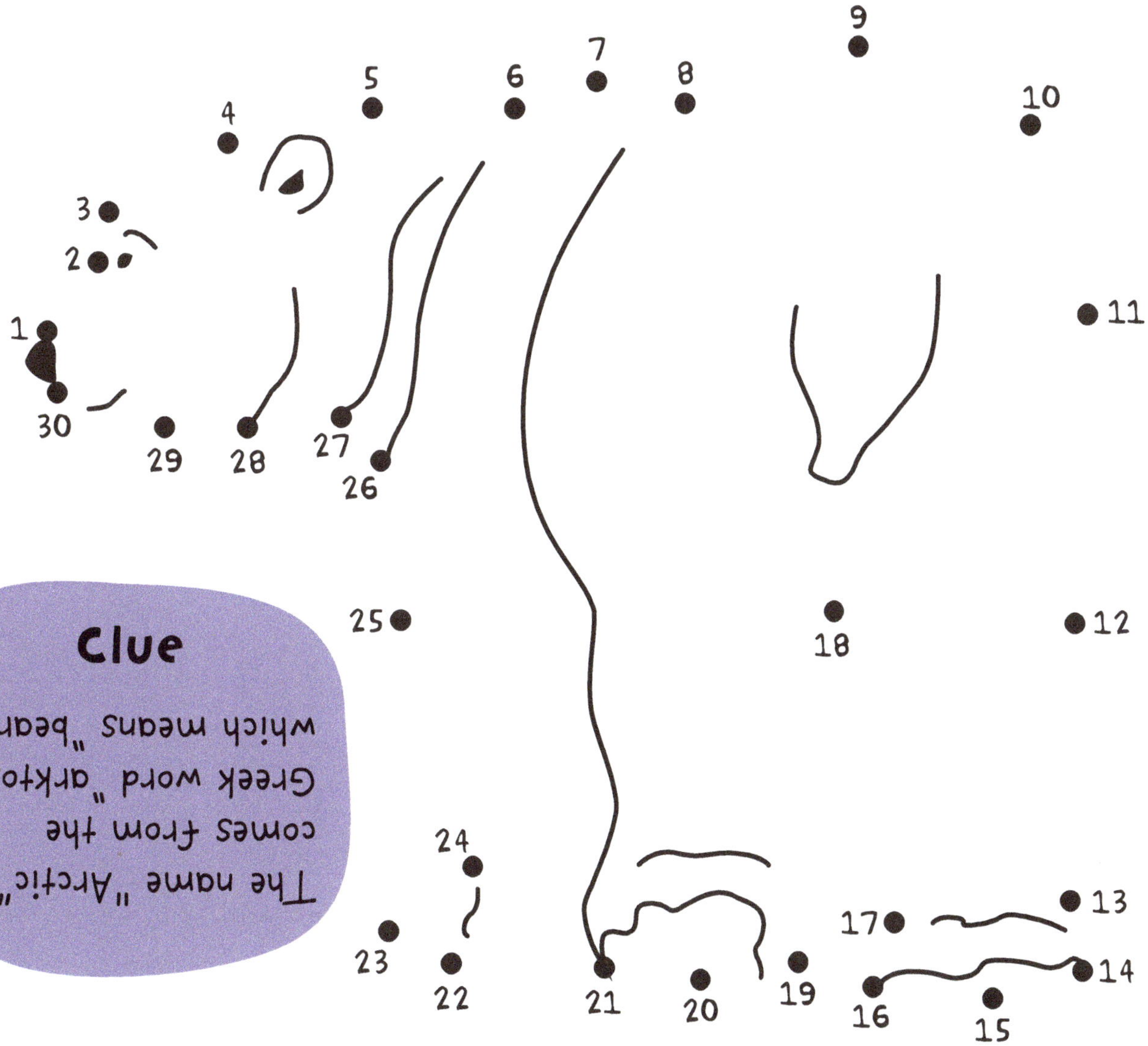

Clue

The name "Arctic" comes from the Greek word "arktos," which means "bear."

The Arctic

The Arctic is the area above the Arctic Circle. The Arctic Circle is an imaginary line around the top of the globe. It is very cold there. The temperature in winter is usually around -22° Fahrenheit (-30° Celsius).

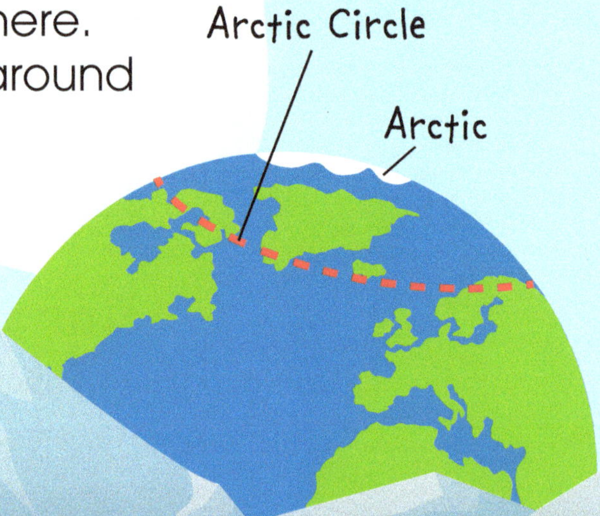

There is no land under the Arctic ice. To prove it, in 1958 the USS *Nautilus* submarine sailed right underneath it!

Because of the way Earth tilts, there are days in winter when the sun never comes up and days in summer when the sun never goes down!

Polar bears don't sleep through winter like other bears. They have their cubs then. Can you help this polar bear mom find her cub?

What Animals Live in the Arctic?

Polar Bear

Polar bears live on land and on floating ice.

Arctic Fox

Arctic foxes live in dens dug into the Arctic snow.

Caribou

Caribou head to the Arctic in the spring.

Puffin

Arctic puffins spend most of their lives at sea.

Beluga Whale

These white whales live in the Arctic Ocean.

Which animal does NOT belong in the freezing Arctic?

a

b

c

Color It In

Copy, print, or trace this picture if you are sharing this book.

Adaptable Animals

Many Arctic animals have slowly changed over time. Slowly changing to adapt to a habitat is known as evolution. Parent animals pass down helpful traits to their young. Young without those traits are more likely to die. Gradually, all the animals in that habitat develop the helpful traits.

fox

Which of these foxes would be best at hiding in the snow?

Arctic fox

Helpful Traits in the Arctic

Big feet give a better grip on the ice.

Small ears and noses have less chance of being damaged by cold.

Being white helps Arctic animals hide from predators and prey.

A thick layer of fat and fur keeps them warm.

Spot the Difference

Each animal in the first picture has a relative in the second picture. The Arctic relatives are well hidden in the snowy habitat. Can you find them all?

The Arctic Ocean

Most of the Arctic Ocean is covered in thick ice. Little sunlight reaches the water below. You wouldn't think anything could live in the cold, dark water. However, amazingly, many animals call the ocean their home.

Can you spot...

- 2 polar bears
- 3 sharks
- 4 seals
- 5 fish

Polar bears and seals are happy on land, too. In the ocean, they must come to the surface to breathe.

Who Eats Who in the Arctic?

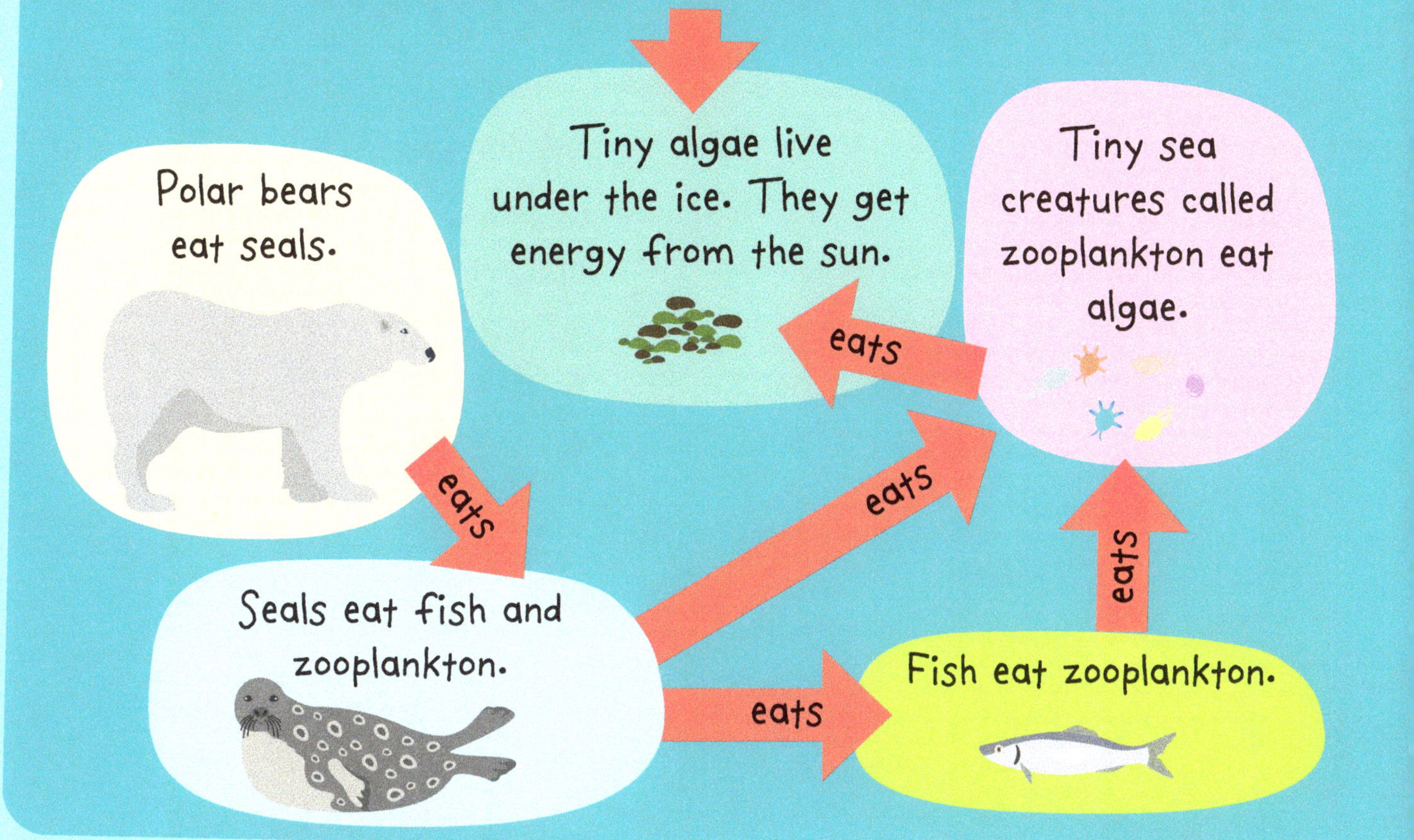

Big, Blubbery Walruses

Atlantic walruses live in the Arctic. Walruses are a little like giant seals, with large tusks. They swim underwater using their flippers. A layer of fat called blubber keeps them warm in the ice-cold ocean. They eat shellfish, such as clams and mussels.

Walruses use their tusks to pull themselves onto the ice.

If they swim long distances under the ice, they break breathing holes in the ice with their tusks.

To sleep in the ocean, walruses fill their cheek pockets with air. These air-filled floats help them keep their nose above water while they sleep.

How Does Blubber Keep a Walrus Warm?

You will need: ice, a bowl, cold water, shortening, a plastic bag

1. Pour cold water and ice into the bowl. Test the water with your finger. Is it very cold?
2. Smear your hand with a thick layer of shortening. This fat acts like walrus blubber.
3. Place your hand in the plastic bag, then place it in the water. Does your hand feel as cold as when you tested the water with your finger? The fat layer should keep it warm.

Draw a Walrus

Can you draw this walrus step-by-step on a separate sheet of paper?

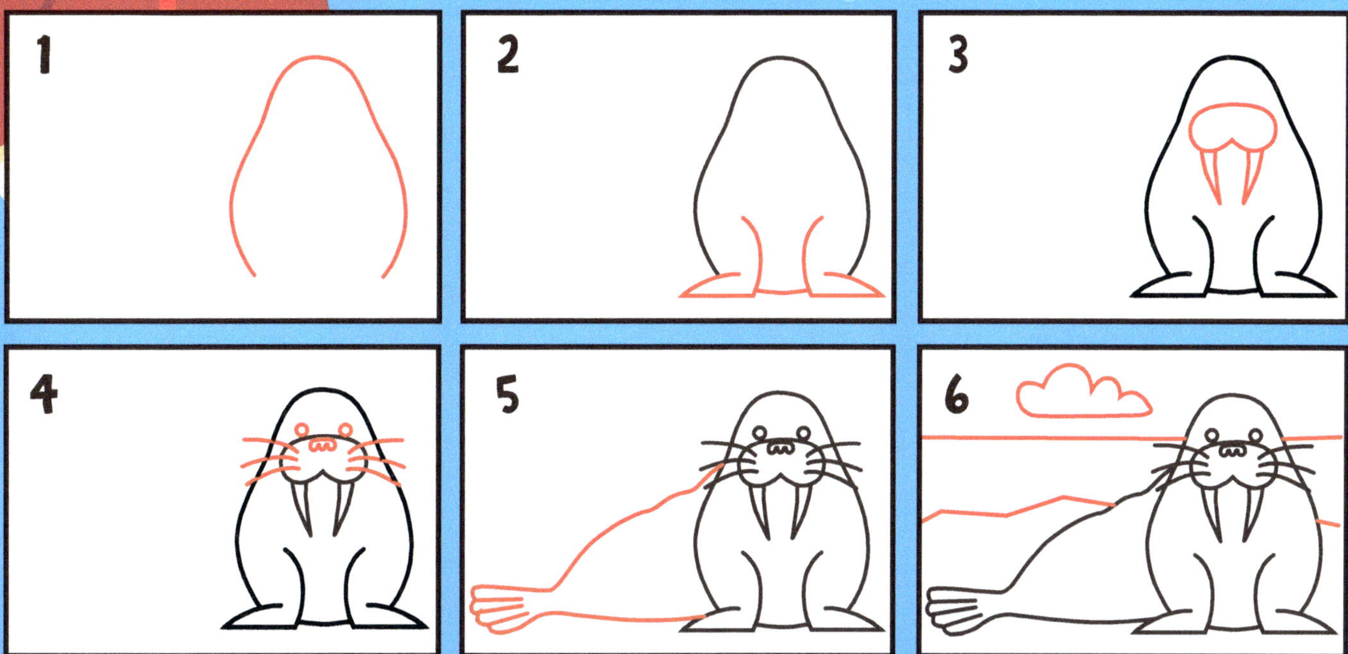

Summer and Winter

The North and South Pole have two seasons—summer and winter. When the poles tilt away from the sun, they have their winter. When they tilt toward the sun, they have their summer. In a polar summer, the sun shines all the time for several months. However, the sun never gets high enough to make the land warm.

Why Do Poles Get 24 Hours of Daylight?

You will need: an orange, a skewer, a flashlight

1. Ask an adult to help push the skewer through the orange.
2. Hold the orange at around a 23.5-degree angle. That is the angle Earth spins at.
3. Shine the flashlight at the orange. Spin the orange around the skewer. When the North Pole is angled toward the flashlight, it is always lit up. The South Pole is always in darkness.

In winter, the sun doesn't rise at all. It is dark all the time for several months. Strong winds make it feel even colder.

An amazing natural light show happens in winter at the poles. The sun creates a kind of energy called solar wind. That energy causes particles in the sky to appear as colors! Oxygen particles make red and green light. Nitrogen particles make blue light.

Shapes in the Dark

Can you tell what North or South Pole animals these silhouettes are? Write your answers on a separate sheet of paper.

Arctic Whales

The Arctic is home to some unusual whales!

Narwhals are known as the unicorns of the sea because of their one long tusk.

Beluga whales have a lump on their forehead. They use the lump to make clicking sounds. The sounds bounce off objects, helping the beluga find things in the dark water.

Bowhead whales use their big heads to break through thick sea ice. These huge, heavy whales can jump high out of the water!

What's Missing?

Look at this orca. It has something the three whales don't have.
Can you see what it is? Can you think why those whales don't have them?

orca

bowhead whale beluga whale narwhal

Hunting Skills

Polar bears are good swimmers, but they are not as fast as the seals they hunt. To catch a seal, they patiently wait by a hole in the ice. When a seal comes up for air, they try to grab it!

Orcas sometimes hunt in groups. They create waves to try to knock seals off the ice.

POLAR BEAR FACTS

- Polar bears are the largest meat eaters on Earth.
- They have black skin.
- Their fur looks white, but the hairs are actually hollow and see-through.
- Polar bears have an incredible sense of smell.

Arctic Hunters Quiz

Can you answer these questions about polar hunters?

1. What color is a polar bear's fur?
2. Can polar bears swim?
3. How do polar bears catch seals?
4. How do orcas sometimes catch seals?

Help this seal pup swim between the ice to reach its mom. Don't go near any orcas or polar bears!

Summer Tundra

The land that circles the Arctic is called tundra. Tundra is icy cold in winter. In summer, the ice melts. This allows some plants to grow. Animals such as caribou, lemmings, and Arctic hare graze on the plants. The soil below stays frozen all year.

Lemmings are small, mouse-like rodents. They live in underground burrows. Their thick fur helps keep them warm. Tundra lemmings have red and brown fur. Arctic lemmings have white fur. Lemmings move from place to place in large groups.

Word Scramble

Unscramble the circles of letters to find three tundra animals. Write your answers on a separate sheet of paper.

1) R O B C I A U

_ _ _ _ _ _ _

2) I L M E N G M

_ _ _ _ _ _ _

3) R I T C C A   A E R H

_ _ _ _ _ _   _ _ _ _

Big, Hairy Cattle

Yaks and musk oxen live in different places, but they have some things in common. They are both related to cattle, eat plants, and have two layers of thick hair to keep them warm.

Yaks live on tundra high in the snowy Himalaya mountains. They have long, thick hair on top of a soft undercoat of short fur. At night and in snowstorms, yaks huddle together to keep each other warm.

Musk oxen live in the Arctic and tundra. They use their hooves to dig for roots, moss, and lichen to eat. Their long, shaggy hair keeps them warm. In summer, they shed their warm undercoat.

Color It In

Copy, print, or trace this picture if you are sharing this book.

Do Layers Keeps You Warmer?

You will need: three jars with lids, cotton balls, a pair of thick socks, some water

1. Fill all three jars halfway with warm water. Put on the lids.
2. Place one jar in a thick sock.
3. Place cotton balls in the toe of the other sock. Put a jar in the sock. Place a layer of cotton balls all around the jar.
4. Place all three jars in the refrigerator.
5. After half an hour, open the three jars and test the water temperature. Which is warmest? Which is coldest?

The jar with two layers around it will probably be warmest. Warm air gets trapped between the layers.

The Antarctic

The Antarctic is home to the South Pole. Unlike the Arctic, the Antarctic has rocky land underneath its thick layer of ice.

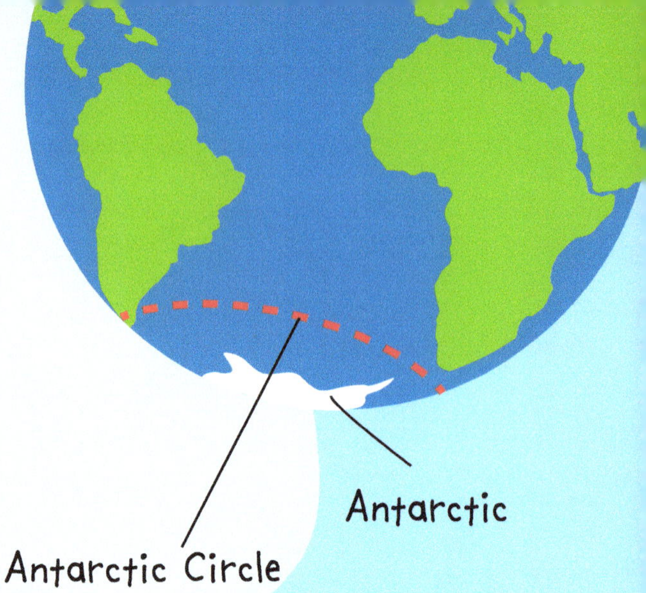

Penguins

Penguins are the only birds that swim but can't fly!

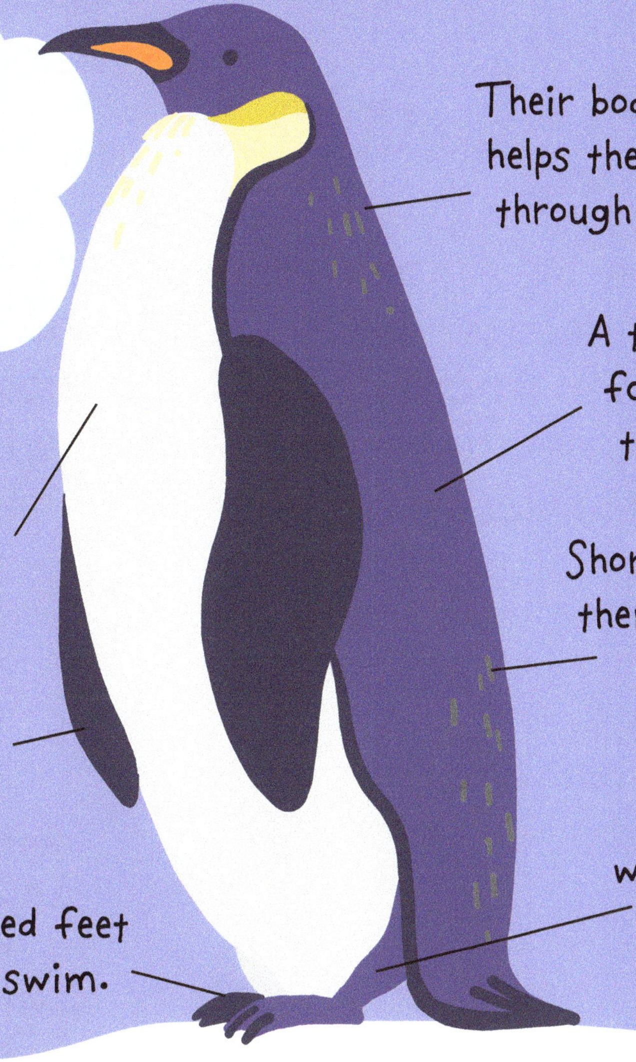

B	P	A	K	Z	W	S	W	H	A
L	F	E	N	O	G	B	H	L	N
G	E	A	N	N	C	X	A	O	T
Y	C	S	A	G	U	L	L	S	A
E	I	P	O	N	U	O	E	U	R
O	D	R	R	M	P	I	H	R	C
R	C	W	P	L	S	T	N	L	T
A	W	O	C	E	A	N	X	A	I
B	S	P	H	N	E	S	R	E	C
U	A	L	B	A	T	R	O	S	S

Word Search

Find these TEN words related to the Antarctic.

PENGUIN
ICE
SEAL
WHALE
ALBATROSS
ORCA
GULL
OCEAN
ANTARCTIC
SNOW

An Icy Desert

Did you know the Antarctic and parts of the Arctic are actually deserts? The Antarctic is the largest desert on Earth. It hardly ever rains or snows there. A desert is somewhere that gets less than 10 inches (25.4 cm) of rain or snow a year.

Scientists believe it hasn't snowed or rained in some places for 14 million years!

Antarctic ice is over 2.5 miles (4 km) thick in some places. The weather is too cold for the ice to melt.

Wind speeds in the Antarctic can reach over 198 miles per hour (320 km/h). Not much can grow in this harsh weather.

Can you find two baby seals in the windy Antarctic?

If all the ice at the Antarctic melted, the sea would rise by around 200 feet (61 m)!

Connect the Dots

The Antarctic fur seal doesn't mind the cold. It is so furry, it has to take mud baths in the summer to cool down! It can turn its back flippers around to help it walk on land. It has cute ears, too! Connect the dots to see what it looks like.

Print or trace this picture and then connect the dots if you are sharing this book.

Color It In

The Southern Ocean

The Southern Ocean surrounds the Antarctic. It is also known as the Antarctic Ocean. Several types of whales, seals, penguins, and squid live in the cold water.

Southern Ocean Sudoku

Each red square, row, and column must have each of these four different creatures from the Southern Ocean. Can you find the missing ones? Write your answers on a separate sheet of paper.

1. 2. 3. 4.

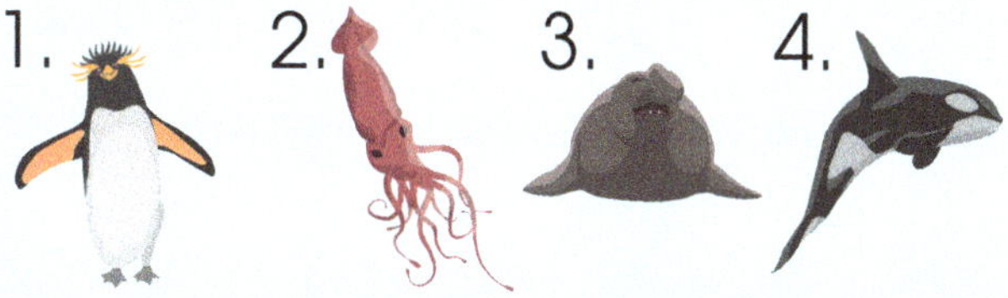

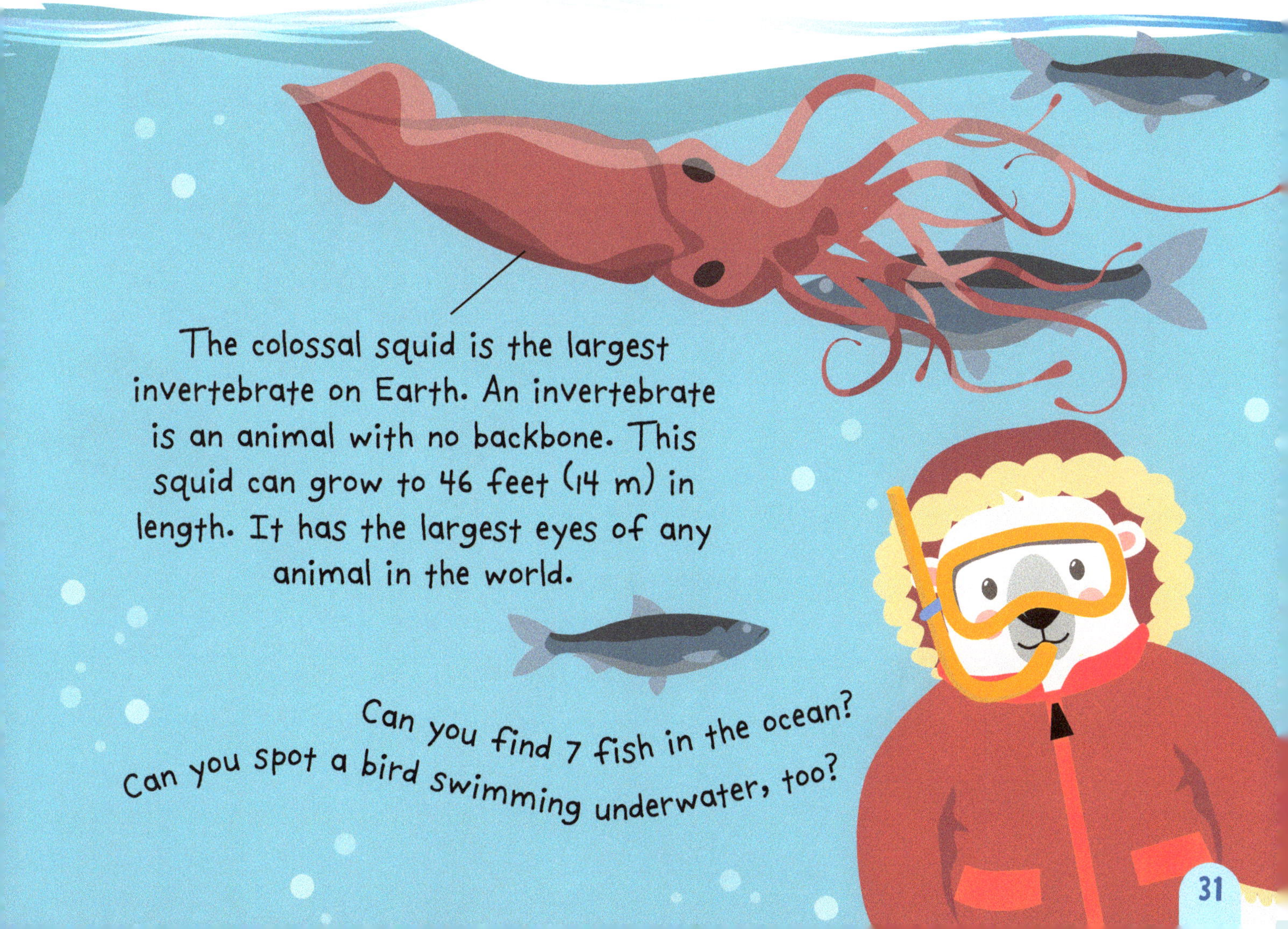

The colossal squid is the largest invertebrate on Earth. An invertebrate is an animal with no backbone. This squid can grow to 46 feet (14 m) in length. It has the largest eyes of any animal in the world.

Can you find 7 fish in the ocean?
Can you spot a bird swimming underwater, too?

Polar Science Stations

No one lives permanently in the Antarctic. Science stations there are visited by thousands of scientists, though. Scientists might study changes to the climate or the animals that live there.

Strengthened icebreaker ships carve paths through the ice in summer.

Dress for the Antarctic!

Antarctic animals have layers of fat, fur, or feathers to keep them warm. Point to the clothes you would pack for a trip to the Antarctic.

Antarctic scientists pack sunglasses. Why? To protect their eyes from the sun's glare reflecting off the dazzling-white ice.

Great Penguin Dads

An Emperor penguin dad is amazing! The female lays a single egg. Then she heads off to sea to feed. The male looks after the egg for over two months. He and the other penguin dads often huddle together to stay warm. They take turns standing on the chilly outer edge of the huddle.

The female penguin returns just as the egg hatches. She cares for the chick while the male heads to the ocean to feed. Then, the pair takes turns caring for the chick. They keep it warm and feed it chewed-up krill, fish, and squid.

Color It In

Blue Whales

The blue whale is the largest mammal on Earth. They live in every ocean. They prefer cool oceans because they find the most food there. They eat tiny shrimplike animals called krill.

A mammal is an animal that breathes air, has a backbone, and feeds its young on milk.

Every 10 to 20 minutes, the whale comes to the surface to breathe.

A blue whale is as long as a 10-story building is high!

Blue whales catch krill in their toothless mouth. Bristles in their mouth called baleen keep the krill from escaping. They push the water out using their tongue.

krill

Blue whales can eat 40 million krill per day!

Underwater Whale Noises

Blue whales talk to each other. They can hear each other's noises 1,000 miles (1,610 km) away. Try this experiment to see how well sound travels underwater, and find out why we don't hear the whales' noises.

You will need: a bathtub, two spoons

With your head out of the water, tap the spoons together under the water. Can you hear them? Now put your ears under the water. Tap the spoons together again. Sound waves travel five times faster through water. Sounds made underwater stay underwater, though. Very little sound passes from water to air.

Humpback Whales

Humpback whales often use their powerful tail to launch themselves out of the water. They twist in midair and come crashing down with a huge splash. This is known as "breaching."

Every humpback whale's fluke is slightly different, like a fingerprint. Can you match the pairs of flukes below?

Whales slap the water with their flukes. This can send signals to other whales. They also tail-slap the water to stun fish. Stunned fish are easier to catch and eat!

Glaciers and Icebergs

Glaciers are areas of dense ice that form on land. They form when layers of snow press down on the layers below. The world's largest glacier is in the Antarctic. It is 250 miles (400 km) long and 60 miles (100 km) wide! Icebergs are chunks of ice that break off from glaciers.

Did you know that glaciers store 75 percent of Earth's fresh water?

A glacier's weight and the force of gravity cause it to move VERY slowly downward.

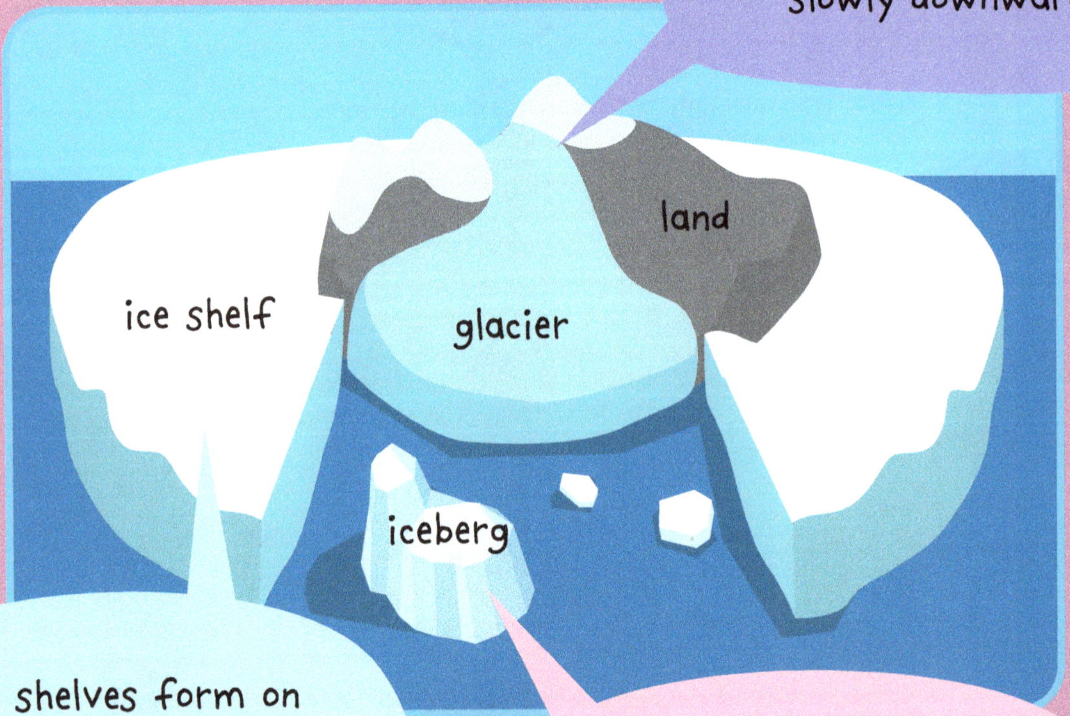

Ice shelves form on the ocean. These walls of ice help keep the glacier from flowing into the ocean.

If a glacier reaches the ocean, large chunks known as icebergs break off and float away.

Make a Marshmallow Glacier

You will need: four marshmallows, a heavy object

1. Balance two marshmallows on top of each other. Your marshmallows represent layers of snow. Place the heavy object on top.
2. After a few minutes, take off the weight. What has happened to the marshmallows?
3. Place two more marshmallows on top. Replace the weight.

The marshmallows should have flattened and spread. No longer fluffy like snow, they will have become more solid, like ice.

Most of an iceberg is under the water. See for yourself! Float an ice cube in a glass of water. Only the very top will be above the water line!

Count the rectangles in this picture. How many are above the water? How many are under the water?

Things float if they are less dense than water. Ice only JUST floats because it is only 9 percent less dense than water.

Protect the Poles!

Earth's climate is changing. This is causing the temperature to get warmer. As the oceans get warmer, the Arctic and Antarctic ice is beginning to melt.

The sun melts the ice.

Animals that live on the ice have less space. They can't hunt on the sea ice for their food.

Sea levels are rising as the melting ice flows into the oceans.

Snow and ice reflect heat from the sun back into space. If the ice disappears, our planet will get even warmer.

Engine and fire fumes can pollute snow. Polluted snow is less able to reflect sunlight, too.

Melting Poles Experiment

You will need: a small freezer-safe bowl, a slightly larger bowl, water, some plastic animals, a ruler

1. Place some water in a bowl and freeze it overnight.
2. Put some water in the larger bowl. Remove the ice block from your frozen bowl. Place it in the water. Place some polar bears and penguins on the ice.
3. Measure the height of the water every half an hour.

What happened to the water level?
What happened to the ice block and the animals?

How You Can Help

- Find out about climate change.
- Eat less meat.
- Plant a tree.
- Recycle.
- Use less fuel and electricity.

HOW? - Walk and cycle more.
- Unplug things you are not using.
- Turn down the heat.

Polar Biome Genius Test

Are you an Arctic and Antarctic genius? Answer these questions to find out.

1 Which animal would survive best in the ice and snow?

a) an animal with thick red fur

b) an animal with thick white fur

c) an animal with no fur or feathers

2 Where is the North Pole?

a) in the Arctic b) in the Antarctic

3 What is wrong with this picture of the Antarctic?

4 In a polar summer, the sun shines all day and all night.

True or false?

5 How does a walrus sleep in the ocean?

a) They never sleep.

b) They go to the bottom of the ocean and find a comfortable rock.

c) They fill their cheeks with air so their head floats and they can breathe.

6 How much of an iceberg is under the water?

a) 10 percent

b) 0 percent

c) 90 percent

Answers

Page 5: The Arctic is named after the polar bear. The Greek word "arktos" means "bear."

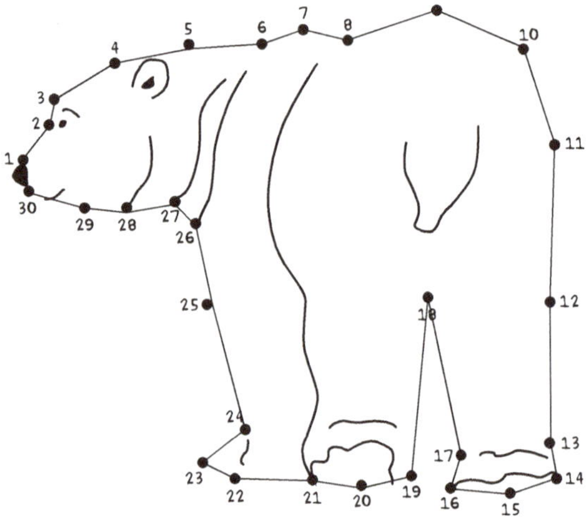

Page 5:

Page 9: b - the cow does not belong in the Arctic.

Page 10: The Arctic fox would be best at hiding in the snow.

Page 11: The relatives are circled in the same color.

Page 12:

Page 17: a) caribou, b) seal, c) penguin

Page 19: The orca has a dorsal fin on the top of its body. Because the other whales swim under the ice, the dorsal fin would get in the way.

Page 21: Quiz: 1) A polar bear's fur is see-through. 2) Yes, polar bears can swim. 3) Polar bears catch seals by waiting by an air hole. 4) Orcas sometimes knock seals off the ice by creating waves with their tails.

Page 21 bottom:

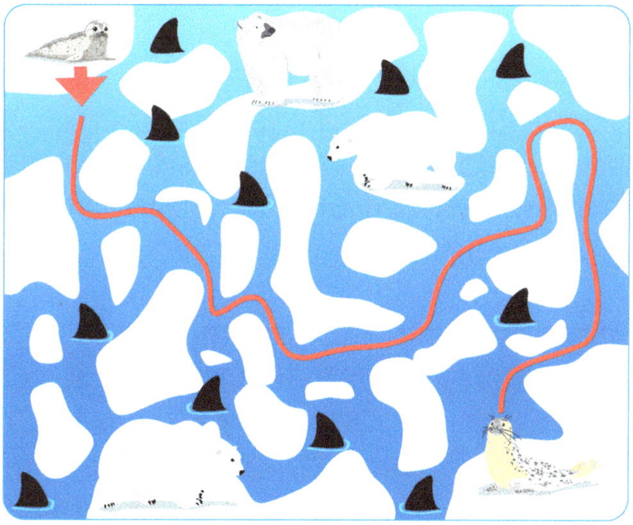

Page 22:

Page 23: 1) caribou, 2) lemming, 3) Arctic hare

Page 27:

B	P	A	K	Z	W	S	W	H	A
L	F	E	N	O	G	B	H	L	N
G	E	A	X	N	C	X	A	O	T
Y	C	S	A	G	U	L	L	S	A
E	I	P	O	N	U	O	E	U	R
O	D	R	R	M	P	I	H	R	C
R	C	W	P	L	S	T	N	L	T
A	W	O	C	E	A	N	X	A	I
B	S	P	H	N	E	S	R	E	C
U	A	L	B	A	T	R	O	S	S

Page 28:

Page 29:

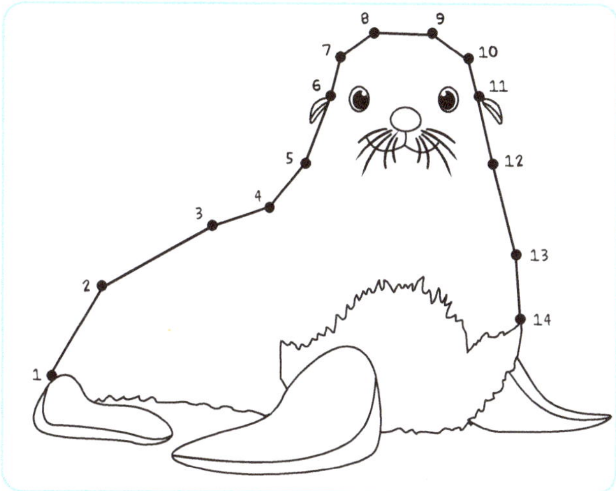

Page 31: a=4, b=1, c=3, d=2

Page 30-31:

Page 33:

Page 35:

Page 39:

Page 41: One rectangle was above the water. Nine rectangles were below the water. This shows that 90 percent of an iceberg is underwater.

Page 43: As the ice melts, the water level will rise. The ice block will disappear, and the animals will fall into the water.

Page 44: 1) b - an animal with thick white fur 2) a - in the Arctic 3) There are no polar bears in the Antarctic. 4) True, in a polar summer the sun will shine all day and all night. 5) c - Walruses fill their cheeks with air so their head floats and they can breathe. 6) c - 90 percent